ONE WORLD

CHURCH

GARY GIBBS

One Christmas, a rabbi from Russia visited an American family as part of a cultural exchange program. His host family wanted to treat him to a new culinary experience, so they took him out one evening to their favorite Chinese restaurant. After the meal, the Chinese waiter brought each of them a little

Christmas gift. It was a small, brass Christmas tree ornament that was stamped with the words "Made in India."

They all laughed at the irony of receiving a "Made in India" gift from a Chinese restaurant. But suddenly, everyone stopped chuckling when they noticed tears rolling down the rabbi's cheeks. Had they offended him in some way?

"Nyet," the rabbi replied. "I was shedding tears of joy to be in a country in which a Buddhist gives a Jew a Christmas gift made by a Hindu."[1]

Such peaceful co-existence and affirmation doesn't happen often between religious faiths. Even today, religious differences frequently escalate into fierce war. It's no wonder that many people want to dismantle the religious "Berlin Wall" that exists between faiths.

In no other community is this truer than within Christianity. Even though all Christian churches profess faith in Jesus as the Son of God, they have not been able to find a way to form a single, united group. For nearly two thousand years, doctrinal differences have splintered Christians into hundreds of independent denominations. But many within Christianity desire to reverse this.

Foremost in the crusade for Christian reunification is the pope. During the last few years he has been doing all he can to pave the way for a single world church. Vatican spokesman Joaquin Navarro-Valls reports that the pope "is pushing hard on the accelerator toward unity." [2]

One of the road signs along the pope's autobahn to unity are his confessions to non-Catholics. While conducting Mass in the Czech Republic, Pope John Paul II said, "Today, I, the pope of the church of Rome, in the name of all Catholics, ask forgiveness for the wrongs inflicted on non-Catholics during the turbulent history of these peoples." [3]

And this isn't the only confession. He is also trying to bridge the gap between the Catholic and Orthodox churches. He says, "men of both sides were to blame" for the conflict that erupted between their churches in the 11th century. [4]

The pope's confessions have found a favorable response. Pennsylvania State University professor William Petersen remarks: "He's *building on sand* [handwritten note]

bringing the church into the 20th century. You've had statements from the early popes that the Roman Church can never err."[5]

Pope John Paul II is not only making verbal overtures; he has also committed himself in print in three highly publicized works. In his letter "Orientale Lumen" ("The Light of the East") he writes: "The sin of our separation is very serious. … How can we be fully credible if we stand divided?" "These divisions must give way to rapprochement and harmony. The wounds on the path of Christian unity must be healed."[6]

But not only on a Bible Foundation — or you are [handwritten note in left margin]

The twelfth encyclical of John Paul's papacy is dedicated to the subject of Christian reunification and is appropriately entitled "Ut Unum Sint" ("May They All Be One"). The pope calls it his "contribution to this most noble goal," which is "to increase the unity of all Christians until they reach full communion."[7]

And in his book *Crossing the Threshold of Hope,* John Paul says it is his desire to see Christian unity achieved within the next few years—before we reach the new millennium. "By the year 2000 we need to be more united, more willing to advance along the path toward the unity for which Christ prayed on the eve of His passion."[8]

Without question, a united Christian church is a very worthy goal. It was Jesus' great burden just before He died. He prayed, "Neither pray I for these alone, but for them also which shall believe on me through their word; That they all may be one; as thou, Father, art in me, and I in thee, that they also may be one in us: that the world may believe that thou hast sent me" (John 17:20, 21).

While none should fault the pope for seeking unity, several questions must be carefully considered. What is the true source of disunity within the Christian church? One Vatican insider suggests, "The main obstacle is not doctrine, but history with all its prejudices."[9]

But is this an accurate evaluation? Do the differences stem merely from prejudice, or is it doctrinal? And, if it is doctrinal, which doctrines are in question? Furthermore, where Catholic, Protestant, and Orthodox doctrines differ, which body will adjust their beliefs to appease the others? And most important of all, how does the Bible instruct God's people to achieve true unity?

The pope is already anticipating some of these questions. In "Ut Unum Sint," he identifies five key doctrines that need further study before we "reach full communion": the relationship of Scripture and tradition, the church's authority, the ordination of priests, the sacrament of the Eucharist, and the role of the Virgin Mary. [10] While this is a good start, there are numerous other areas that must also be covered before unity of any degree can be reached. But for now, let's briefly look at each of these five doctrines to see what the Catholic Church teaches and what must transpire if a united world church is ever to become more than a dream in the night.

Scripture Versus Tradition

Admiral Byrd, the famous explorer, knows death is only minutes away. He's caught outside in an unforgiving blizzard at the South Pole. Snow swirls around him like a dancing sheet. The temperature, well below zero, chills him to the bone. His limbs stiffen and threaten to freeze. The cold is painful.

But all is not hopeless. He knows that he is within 100 yards of the warmth and security of his hut. But how to find the hut is the problem. Everywhere he looks there is the same snow and ice. White. Everything is white. There isn't a single landmark. If only he could find one to use as a central reference point, then he could navigate to find the hut. But without it, he might head in the wrong direction to certain death. "A man can't last long out here," he thinks.

Byrd knows there is no time for panic. Calmly he assesses the situation. In his hand is the 10-foot pole he always carries. It is his only chance. He sticks the pole in the snow and then ties his brightly colored scarf to it. Then he strikes out to find his hut, first in one direction and then in another—but always keeping the pole with the waving scarf in sight. Three times he returns to the pole, and on the fourth excursion he discovers his hut and stumbles into its warmth.

Our world is like trackless Antarctica in a blizzard. The devil blinds the minds of humanity "lest the light of the glorious gospel of Christ ... should shine unto them" (2 Corinthians 4:4). We are lost in sin, but there is a place of safety—heaven. It is out there. And it is not too far distant. That is, if a person can find the straight and narrow path that leads to it.

Just how do we find this path? We need a reference point. We need an inerrant guide that can lead us through all the twists and turns and the ups and downs of life. But there is one danger. If the thing we use as our reference point slips either to the left or to the right, then we are sure to stray and die.

Catholic and Protestant churches have disputed the identity of this reference point for centuries. The Catholic Church teaches that the guide to heaven consists of the Bible and nearly two thousand years of church tradition. "We find the truths revealed by God in Sacred Scripture and Sacred Tradition. ... Both Sacred Scripture and Sacred Tradition are the inspired word of God, and both are forms of divine revelation." [11]

Protestants, however, believe the Bible alone must form the basis for faith and practice. In fact, this was a major issue in the Protestant split from the Catholic Church in the 15th century. John Wycliffe, John Huss, Jerome, Martin Luther, and many other Protestants began as faithful Catholics. But while in pursuit of a closer relationship with God they discovered the practices of their church often contradicted the clear teachings of the Bible.

The ensuing conflict was more than a battle of ideologies. These men had tried to live by the authority of tradition and personally found it bankrupt. Luther had a tortured conscience. Painful penances and fastings threatened to rob him of life itself. He didn't find peace until he discovered the plan of salvation clearly presented in the Bible as a gift to all who believe. Somehow the traditions of the church had obliterated this most vital truth. For centuries it taught that salvation could be had by penance, pilgrimage, and payment. Salvation by faith as the free gift of God had been completely forgotten. Clearly tradition and Scripture were at odds—a fact that was not lost on the Protestants. A fact for which Luther was willing to die.

In Worms, Germany, Luther stood before an august assembly of bishops, prelates, priests, and noble men to answer for his strange "new" doctrine of salvation as a free gift to those who accept Christ as their Savior. When commanded to renounce his "heretical" teachings, he said, at peril to his life, "Unless I am refuted and convicted by testimonies of the Scriptures or by clear arguments (since I believe neither the pope nor the councils alone, it being evident that they have often erred and contradicted themselves), I am conquered by the Holy Scriptures quoted by me, and my conscience is bound in the Word of God, I can not and will not recant anything, since it is unsafe and dangerous to do anything against the conscience. Here I stand. God help me." [12] Tradition or Scripture. Luther had drawn the Mason-Dixon line for the Protestant Reformation.

In 1545, the Catholic Church finally convened the Council of Trent in Austria to answer the questions raised by the Protestants. What will it be, tradition or Scripture? The answer came near the conclusion of the meetings. "Finally, at the last opening on the eighteenth of January, 1562, all hesitancy was set aside. The archbishop of Reggio made a speech in which he openly declared that tradition stood above Scripture. The authority of the church could not therefore be bound to the authority of the Scriptures." [13]

Like a sledgehammer striking a wedge in a block of dry wood, a split was created that has never been mended. But now, nearly four hundred and fifty years later, the pope is calling for reunification. And he accurately states that this issue of Scripture versus tradition must be resolved.

So what is correct? Is it Scripture and tradition, or Scripture alone? Certainly the best source for an objective answer to this dilemma is the Word of God itself. What does the Bible say about tradition?

It teaches several things. First, traditions that are in harmony with God's Word are to be respected. "Therefore, brethren, stand fast, and hold the traditions which ye have been taught, whether by word, or our epistle" (2 Thessalonians 2:15).

Secondly, not all traditions are pleasing to God. "Howbeit in vain do they worship me, teaching for doctrines the commandments of men. ... Full well ye reject the commandment of God, that ye may keep your own tradition" (Mark 7:7–9). Traditions that replace God's commandments are vain worship. They reveal contempt for God's authority.

Lastly, God has promised to rid His church of unscriptural traditions. "Thus have ye made the commandment of God of none effect by your tradition." "Every plant, which my heavenly Father hath not planted, shall be rooted up" (Matthew 15:6, 13).

We cannot depend upon the traditions of men. They are often an erring guide. And not surprisingly so. Humans are erring. Even while trying our best, we make mistakes of mammoth proportion.

For centuries Protestant churches have claimed that Catholicism follows numerous unscriptural traditions. Is this charge accurate? If you are a Catholic, this question is doubly important. You love God and desire to please Him. But fellow believers say that many of your church's doctrines are not found in the Bible. Your pope also acknowledges that this is a serious issue that needs study. And he says it must be resolved if we are to answer Jesus' prayer for unity among Christians.

Therefore, you will want to ask yourself this very important question. Does the Catholic Church really have many unscriptural traditions? Yes, unfortunately it does. This may be hard to accept, but it is true. Cardinal John Henry Newman made this candid admission: "The use of temples, and these dedicated to particular saints, and ornamented on occasions with branches of trees; incense, lamps, and candles; votive offerings on recovery from illness; holy water; asylums; holy days and seasons, use of calendars, processions, blessings on the fields; sacerdotal vestments, the tonsure, the ring in marriage, turning to the east, images at a later date, perhaps the ecclesiastical chant, and the Kyrie Eleison ... *are all of pagan origin,* and sanctified by their adoption into the Church" (emphasis mine).[14] Many Catholic doctrines are of pagan origin and are not found in the Bible.

But, wait. Catholics need not feel that this is an unkind thrust against them. This is not just a Catholic issue. Protestants also hold many unscriptural traditions that contradict clear teachings of the Bible. This fact has not been missed by some Catholics.

Notice the following Catholic challenge to Protestants to be consistent with their "Scripture alone" maxim. "The Bible does not contain all the teachings of the Christian religion, nor does it formulate all the duties of its members. Take, for example, the matter of Sunday observance, the attendance at divine services and the abstention from unnecessary servile work on that day, a matter upon which our Protestant neighbors have for many years laid great emphasis. Let me address myself to my dear non-Catholic reader:

"You believe that the Bible alone is a safe guide in religious matters. You also believe that one of the fundamental duties enjoined upon you by your Christian faith is that of Sunday observance. But where does the Bible speak of such an obligation? I have read the Bible from the first verse of Genesis to the last verse of Revelation, and have found no reference to the duty of sanctifying the Sunday. The day mentioned in the Bible is not the Sunday, the first day of the week but the Saturday, the last day of the week.

"It was the Apostolic Church [i.e. Catholic Church] which ... changed the observance to the Sunday. ... In observing the Sunday as you do, is it not apparent that you are really acknowledging the insufficiency of the Bible alone as a rule of faith and religious conduct, and proclaiming the need of a divinely established teaching authority which in theory you deny?" [15]

John A. O'Brien's logic is glaringly accurate. If Protestants are going to insist that Catholics return to the Bible, then they must do the same. And back to the Bible we all must go—Catholics *and* Protestants.

God's Word is the only true foundation for consensus of faith. Catholics must stop defending their position that tradition and Scripture are of equal authority. And Protestants must surrender their unscriptural traditions and truly live by "every word" of God (Matthew 4:4). We should all keep the Bible's Saturday Sabbath along with every other teaching of God's Word. Only as we Christians are honest with God's truth can we hope to positively impact an unbelieving world for eternal good.

Church Authority

India has a problem. They worship rats. And their worship is literally consuming them. Tens of thousands of rats overrun certain cities. They race across floors; feasting on anything they can sink their teeth into. Rats are especially revered and worshipped at the temple of Karni Mata. Here the furry critters leap onto the platform where food is placed for them. They eat while the priest serenades them with hymns and plays cymbals. These well-cared-for rats reproduce prolifically. And few Indians will kill them, fearing that in so doing they will kill their god's companion.

But the rats have introduced something worse than more rats. They've brought the plague. Hundreds have died as a result. But since the Indians won't kill the varmints, the plague continues to spread.

The issue of what we worship is crucial in all cultures. This is why the Catholic position on the authority of the Church and pope is so sensitive with non-Catholics. Catholic catechisms teach that church authority refers to the infallibility of the pope. "When the pope in his official capacity, with the fullness of his authority, as successor of St. Peter and head of the church on earth, proclaims a doctrine of faith or morals binding on the whole Church, *he is preserved from error.* It is to be noted that three conditions are required: (1) The pope must speak *ex cathedra*, i.e., from the Chair of Peter in his official capacity; (2) The decision must be binding on the whole Church; (3) It must be on a matter of faith or morals" (emphasis mine). [16] These infallible doctrines of the pope are "certainly true and binding in conscience on all the faithful." [17]

So what should we believe regarding the pope's authority? Catholics and Protestants must turn to the Bible to form their opinions. Here we'll find that Scripture teaches no human is infallible. "For all have sinned, and come short of the glory of God" (Romans 3:23). Even those who have been specially called to holy service are fallible. History is an eloquent witness to the foibles of church leaders, including popes. The apostle Peter himself fell into sin numerous times (see Matthew 16:21–23; Luke 22:54–62; and Galatians 2:11–14).

Now, the church must have leaders. But every thing they teach as truth must be tested by Scripture. The Bible never teaches that spiritual leaders have periods where they speak *ex cathedra*. There is no special chair or office from which they can proclaim infallible truth.

But the Bible does tell us to test our leaders by the Word. The believers in Berea were commended for being "more noble than those in Thessalonica, in that they … searched the scriptures daily" to see if Paul's teachings were in accord with God's Word (Acts 17:10, 11).

The Bible also warns us against spiritual leaders who are used by Satan to lead many astray. "Of your own selves shall men arise, speaking perverse things, to draw away disciples after them" (Acts 20:30). Infallibility is a dangerous doctrine. If we ascribe it to any man, we make ourselves very vulnerable to deception. Therefore, "Beloved, believe not every spirit, but try the spirits whether they are of God: because many false prophets are gone out into the world" (1 John 4:1).

How are we to "try the spirits?" Isaiah 8:20 says, "To the law and to the testimony: if they speak not according to this word, it is because there is no light in them." They are to be tested by the Bible. When Paul warned the church to beware of leaders who introduce erroneous teachings, he said to test them by the Word. "And now, brethren, I commend you to God, and to the *word* of his grace, which is able to build you up, and to give you an inheritance among all them which are sanctified" (Acts 20:32 emphasis mine). We can be safe only as we test every declaration of truth by God's Word.

Now the pope may be a good man with noble intentions. Nevertheless, all that he says and advocates must be tested by the Holy Bible. No human has carte blanche infallibility. For centuries, popes have claimed infallibility as direct successors of Peter, who they believe was the first pope. But according to Scripture, Peter was not established as a pope. He wasn't even the leader of the early church councils—James was (see Acts 15:1–22).

Another problem with the papacy is that it runs counter to God's truth. Popes have great power. People bow before them. They confess their sins to them. Popes live amid great pomp, splendor, and riches. They have been some of the most powerful men who have ever lived. But when one studies the Bible for examples of men of God, we find a much humbler model. Our Lord Himself taught that those who desire rich robes and to sit in high places are not following Him (Matthew 23:1–12).

Clearly, the Bible never claims for church leaders what the papacy claims for itself. The papacy, therefore, is an unbiblical position. If consensus of faith is to be achieved, then all Christians will need to get back to the Bible. The claims made regarding the powers and rights of the papacy will need to be officially renounced. The pomp and splendor should also be traded for Jesus' example of humility.

The pope has indicated he is willing to explore some change in the function of the papacy. While not promising to surrender his ultimate authority over the church, he has said that he would seek "to find a way of exercising the primacy which, while in no way renouncing what is essential to its mission, is nonetheless open to a new situation." [18]

What possible new situation could the Vatican be considering? The president of the Vatican's Pontifical Council for the Promotion of Unity of Christians has suggested that the pope may act as a mediator in religious disputes.

Unfortunately, it seems the pontiff is only considering not insisting that Protestants accept the doctrine of papal infallibility. What he will settle for is to be the final mediator in doctrinal disputes between Christians. But this is still unacceptable to those who desire to take their faith from the Bible. No single human can claim the power to be the final word on doctrine and morals. Every believer must study the Scriptures for himself to determine what God would have him do.

When there is a controverted point of doctrine, the question can come to an assembly of representatives of the church for their humble study of God's Word to see what Scripture truly teaches. Many minds working together to find God's will is always a lot safer than one man being in charge of determining truth.

But even in religious assemblies, we see the weakness of man. Many Christian convocations have made declarations that run counter to Bible truth. What should believers do in such cases? They should follow what the Bible teaches. Many American Catholics are already following their own convictions to some degree. Catholicism officially teaches that nearly all forms of birth control are sin. But most American Catholics disagree. Thereby they too deny the absolute, infallible authority of the pope.

The authority of the church is a crucial question, and the pope is correct in tagging it for discussion. But until he reverses the supremacy and primacy of the papacy, apostolic succession, and the authority of the church to be the sole interpreter of Scripture, no unity can be achieved with those believers who want to remain true to the Bible. Christianity cannot unite around a fallible human, no matter how noble a person he may be. Only as we humbly submit ourselves to God and His Word will we be able to come together.

The Ordination of Priests

We now come to the third doctrine identified by Pope John Paul II. What does the Catholic Church teach about the ordination of priests? Official Catholic teaching is that priests are ordained to have the power to forgive sins.[19] Some American Catholics may disagree with this representation. They may be honestly unaware of this doctrine. Nevertheless, it is true. Here are a few excerpts from official Catholic sources.

"An authorized priest … [says] the words 'I absolve you from your sins.' … All bishops and priests have the power to forgive sins or absolve sins." [20]

"Who has the power to forgive sin today? All bishops and priests of the Catholic Church can forgive sin. ... What do you have to do to have your sins forgiven? You have to be truly sorry for them and confess them to a Catholic priest." [21]

Sometimes American Catholics defend the confessional by comparing it to going to a counselor or psychologist. They claim the priest does not actually forgive sins, but simply plays the role of a counselor.

However, when the pope speaks about priests, he refers to the official Catholic position and not the "corrupted," Americanized version. The Church tries to make its official teaching clear in its catechisms. "Does the priest merely pray that your sins will be forgiven? No, acting as God's instrument and ordained minister, he truly forgives the sins." [22] "This is not a mere ritual repetition or psychological exercise." [23] "Does the priest really forgive your sins? ... the priest really forgives your sins. The priest does not merely 'pray away' your sins." [24]

This Catholic teaching is based on John 20:23: "Whosoever sins ye remit, they are remitted unto them; and whosoever sins ye retain, they are retained." A correct understanding of this verse requires reading the context. Before telling the disciples about the remission of sins, Jesus said, "As my Father hath sent me, even so send I you." The disciples were to go to the world in a way similar to which Jesus was sent to our world.

How did the Father send Jesus to our world? Jesus said, "For I have not spoken of myself; but the Father which sent me, he gave me a commandment, what I should say, and what I should speak" (John 12:49). "I do nothing of myself; but as my Father hath taught me, I speak these things" (John 8:28). "I came down from heaven, not to do mine own will, but the will of him that sent me" (John 6:38).

Jesus was sent not to speak His own words or teach His own doctrine or to do His own will. He came to speak the Father's word and will and sent His disciples to do the same. Like an ambassador, the disciples were to tell others about the will and word of the Person they represented. "God ... hath given to us the ministry of reconciliation; To wit, that God was in Christ, reconciling the world unto himself, not imputing their trespasses unto them; and hath committed unto us the *word* of reconciliation. Now then we are ambassadors for Christ, as though God did beseech you by us; we pray you in Christ's stead, be ye reconciled to God" (2 Corinthians 5:18–20, emphasis mine). Notice that the power to actually forgive sins was not given to the disciples as priests, but only the *word* of reconciliation as ambassadors. Ministers and believers can only pass on the word of truth that Jesus has reconciled the sinner to Himself if they will confess and believe upon the Lord Jesus Christ. We have the right to invite and urge people in behalf of Jesus to come to Him. But the actual ability to read the heart and to grant forgiveness is something only the Almighty can do.

So how is it that "whosoever sins ye retain, they are retained"? Whenever an unbeliever does not accept a believer's call to repentance, then we have caused them to retain their sins. "To him that knoweth to do good, and doeth it not, to him it is sin" (1 James 4:17). "If ye were blind, ye should have no sin: but now ye say, We see; therefore your sin remaineth" (John 9:41). Sin remains and is retained when a sinner has encountered truth and has refused to repent and accept it.

So when the disciples took truth to people and they refused to accept it, their sins were retained. "If I had not come and spoken unto them, they had not had sin: but now they have no cloak [margin: excuse] for their sin" (John 15:22). "And whosoever shall not receive you, nor hear your words, when ye depart out of that house or city, shake off the dust of your feet. Verily I say unto you, It shall be more tolerable for the land of Sodom and Gomorrha in the day of judgment, than for that city" (Matthew 10:14, 15). On the other hand, if people accept the good news of salvation in Christ, then their sins are forgiven by God.

Man is on dangerous ground when he tries to usurp God's prerogatives. No one should ever say the words used by the priests in the Catholic sacrament of penance: "I absolve you from your sins." Only God can forgive sin. "Who is this which speaketh blasphemies? Who can forgive sins, but God alone" (Luke 5:21)? "Blasphemy," the Bible calls it. Strong language we would do well to remember!

Sin requires the death penalty be paid. Whenever we sin and confess to God, Jesus applies the blood of His death on the cross to our account. He alone can read the heart and apply the blood accordingly. We do not have this power. We don't know if a person is truly sincere and desirous of transformation. We misjudge others all the time.

There is a danger in accepting humans as our mediators with God. God regards only one Mediator. "For there is one God, and one mediator between God and men, the man Christ Jesus" (1 Timothy 2:5). For humans to take the place of this Mediator is presumptuous. This is trying to take the place of Jesus and God. And no good Catholic or Protestant Christian wants this to happen.

One cannot find any indication within the biblical record that the apostles exercised the authority supposedly conferred upon them to forgive sins. They certainly would have done it if they had understood Jesus' words in the manner the Catholic Church teaches. Neither does the Bible refer to the Catholic Church's confessional. There is no record of sinners going to the apostles to confess their sins and receive forgiveness. Yet, we do read numerous instances of the disciples directing people to God for forgiveness. "Repent therefore of this thy wickedness, and *pray God,* if perhaps the thought of thine heart may be forgiven thee" (Acts 8:22, emphasis mine).

Associated with the ordination of the priest is celibacy. According to the Catholic catechism, "The basis for clerical celibacy is the example of Christ and His apostles." [25] Does the Bible really teach that priests are to remain unmarried and celibate for life? Admittedly, Jesus was celibate. But He did not command this for all who should follow Him in ministry. He called Peter to be an apostle, and Peter was married. "[Peter's] wife's mother lay sick of a fever" (Mark 1:30).

Although it is recommended for those who choose it, celibacy is not a requirement for ministry. Jesus says that there are those who "have made themselves eunuchs for the kingdom of heaven's sake. He that is able to receive it, let him receive it" (Matthew 19:12). The apostle Paul highly recommended celibacy.

He saw it as an opportunity to care only for the things of God (1 Corinthians 7:32). But he also says this is his opinion and not a direct command from God. "I speak this by permission, and not of commandment" (1 Corinthians 7:6). Furthermore, Paul did not forbid marriage. "If thou marry, thou hast not sinned; and if a virgin marry, she hath not sinned" (1 Corinthians 7:28).

The Catholic position is not as flexible as that of Paul. "By Church law a Catholic priest in the western Church is obligated to live a life of celibacy [no marriage]."[26] The dilemma the pope finds himself in is that he forbids that which God clearly permits. Many Catholics, recognizing this, are trying to get their church to change this teaching. But the pope has indicated it will not change.

A church in Georgia once installed chimes to play hymns over a loudspeaker for the townspeople to hear during supper. Every evening the chimes faithfully played their sweet music. But a nearby turkey farmer was not soothed by the sound. It seemed that the chimes disturbed his turkeys during their evening feeding. The birds just wouldn't eat while the music played, and they were not getting fat for the market. Discussions between the farmer and church deteriorated. Pretty soon things became quite ugly. The farmer tried to silence the loudspeaker on the steeple by shooting it. In retaliation church members sneaked into the turkey pens at night, spooking the birds and giving them one more reason not to eat. Only after the birds had a complete nervous breakdown and the church steeple was peppered with bullet holes did the two parties finally come to an agreement that met both their needs. The church played the chimes at a different hour and the farmer called a cease-fire. [27]

Resolving doctrinal differences does not need to become a shouting match and certainly not a shooting match. Both the pope and Protestants agree that the Catholic doctrine of the ordination of priests must be resolved. And it must be done in light of Bible truth. Teachings regarding the priest's ability to forgive sins, apostolic succession, and celibacy will need to be radically changed to come into harmony with the Bible. This is the only wise thing to do if we are to answer Jesus' prayer for Christian unity.

The Eucharist

Four children were born to a family in Amman, Jordan. Each birth certificate said the child was a girl. And for 13 years the family believed this. But when the oldest child reached puberty, "she" started revealing male characteristics. The teenage "girl" grew facial hair, her voice broke, and she developed a male physique. Doctors examining Mohammed diagnosed him with a rare genetic defect that left him appearing to be female when in reality he was male. Apparently, during his development in the womb his male organs never descended.

Mohammed's three younger siblings were also diagnosed with the same defect. Fortunately, all the children were successfully operated on and are now males. The day of their transformation was one of great celebration. The girls, now turned boys, cut their long hair, removed their jewelry, and wore boys' pajamas. And their jubilant grandmother Fatima Netasha said, "I had six granddaughters and two grandsons, and now I have six grandsons and two granddaughters. I thank God and the doctor." [28]

Sometimes things aren't as they appear. This is what is at the heart of the controversy over the Eucharist, or the Lord's Supper. Protestants view the bread and grape juice as *symbols* of Jesus' body and blood. But according to Catholic teaching the bread and wine aren't what they appear to be—mere bread and wine. Instead, they are *literally* the *real* body, blood, and person of Jesus.

Official Catholic teaching is unambiguous. "The Eucharist is a sacrament which really, truly, and substantially contains the body and blood, soul, and divinity of our Lord Jesus Christ under the appearances of bread and wine." [29] "After consecration, this sign contains the whole Christ, his body and blood, his soul and divinity." [30] "Christ is present in the Eucharist ... with all his physical properties, hands and feet and head and human heart. He is present with his human soul, with his thoughts, desires, and human affections." [31]

Another difference between Catholic and Protestant beliefs is that of relevance. Protestants view the service as a holy ritual in which people voluntarily participate. However, the Catholic Church teaches that

"The Eucharist is necessary for salvation."[32] This is because of their view that the benefits of the cross can be had only by partaking of Jesus' "literal" body as found in the bread.

Follow this to its logical conclusion. The only bread that can be Jesus' body is bread that has had the special prayer and blessing of the Catholic priest. No priest means no changing of the bread into the body of Christ. No body of Christ means no salvation. A Protestant pastor cannot do what the Catholic priest can with the bread. Only the priest has the power conferred upon him to command God to come down from heaven and enter the bread. Therefore, if people are going to be saved, they must go to a Catholic Church to receive the Eucharist. Furthermore, in order to receive the Eucharist they must first become a Catholic. "The person who is receiving instructions in preparation for full membership in the Catholic Church should participate in the Mass but may not receive Holy Communion."[33]

What did Jesus mean when He said in Matthew 26:26–28, "Take, eat; this is my body. ... Drink ye all of it; For this is my blood"?

Did He really mean that His literal body and blood were present in the bread and wine? The disciples knew this wasn't what He referred to. They had heard Him speak like this before. Jesus once said, "I am the living bread which came down from heaven: if any man eat of this bread, he shall live forever: and the bread that I will give is my flesh, which I will give for the life of the world. … Except ye eat the flesh of the Son of man, and drink his blood, ye have no life in you" (John 6:51–53).

On that day, many who listened interpreted Jesus' words very literally. They thought He advocated salvation by cannibalism. They were shocked. Jesus knew their thoughts, so He clarified what He meant. "It is the spirit that quickeneth; the flesh profiteth nothing: the words that I speak unto you, they are spirit, and they are life" (John 6:63). Jesus says His life is contained in His words. To eat His Word means to read and meditate upon its meaning. When we apply Jesus' teachings to our life, then we've truly eaten His Word. The Catholic teaching of the Eucharist misses this point. Instead, what Jesus intends to be spiritual is taken literally.

Another controverted point regarding the Eucharist concerns the wine. In the Catholic communion service, only the priests drink it. This teaching came into the Church at the Council of Constance, A.D. 1414–1418, and is not taught in God's Word. When Jesus took the cup, He gave it to *all* those present, saying, "This cup is the new testament in my blood: *this do ye,* as oft as *ye drink it,* in remembrance of me" (1 Corinthians 11:25 emphasis mine; See also Matthew 26:27, 28). The blessing of this service is for every believer, not just priests.

Yes, the pope is right again. The Eucharist needs to be studied. Imagine what blessings can come to Christianity if we all return to Bible truth. United on the clear teachings of God's Word, we can be a powerful witness to unbelievers. But before unity can be reached, we must also resolve another doctrinal difference the pope said must be resolved—the Virgin Mary.

The Virgin Mary

The Lawrence Welk Show had its television premier in 1955 and launched Welk into becoming what *Life* magazine called "the most popular musician in U.S. history." But things weren't always so rosy for Lawrence Welk. Once, after playing his accordion for a dance, he overheard one of the band members remark, "Did you get a load of that accordionist? If I had to play every night with him, I'd go back to jerking sodas." [34] At the time, it appeared Welk might be a failure, but he continued to play and finally landed his television show. Though many would rate him as an average musician, 40 million people tuned in to his program faithfully every Saturday night. Quite a large following for an ordinary musician!

To many Christians, Mary, though extremely blessed to be the mother of Jesus, was still just an ordinary human. In the Catholic Church, however, she "is honored and loved second only to God Himself." [35] Because the pope is well aware that this reverence for Mary is a major block in the road to unity, he has put it on the list for discussion. And Protestants have some very good reasons to raise objections to this Catholic belief.

The Bible is very clear that Jesus is our Savior. No other person can atone for our sins. So to God alone should we pray. It is Jesus "who is even at the right hand of God, who also maketh intercession for us" (Romans 8:34). Yet, Catholic catechisms contain numerous prayers to Mary pleading for her to make intercession for our sins. The very popular Hail Mary prayer says, "Holy Mary, Mother of God, pray for us sinners, now and at the hour of our death."[36]

The Hail Holy Queen prayer addresses Mary as mankind's advocate. "Hail Holy Queen, Mother of Mercy, our life, our sweetness and our hope! To thee do we cry, poor banished children of Eve; to you do we send up our sighs, mourning and weeping in this valley of tears! Turn, then most gracious Advocate, your eyes of mercy towards us, and after this, our exile, show unto us the blessed fruit of thy womb, Jesus. ... O sweet Virgin Mary! Pray for us, o holy Mother of God. That we may be made worthy of the promises of Christ."[37] The Bible, however, says that there is no advocate for man other than Jesus. "We have an advocate with the Father, Jesus Christ the righteous" (1 John 2:1).

The second problem with the Catholic doctrine of Mary is called the Immaculate Conception. This teaches that Mary was "conceived without sin." [38] "Not only was she free from the slightest stain of actual sin, but by a singular miracle of divine grace she was free also from original sin, with which all the other children of Adam are born into this world. It was eminently fitting that she ... should be undefiled by even that slight shadow of Adam's fall. To her alone, among all the members of the race, was granted this singular immunity ... the Immaculate Conception [refers] ... to the conception of Mary in the womb of her mother without the stain of original sin." [39]

Unfortunately, this teaching finds no support in the Bible. It was only recently proclaimed as a dogma of the Catholic faith in 1854. [40] The Bible unequivocally declares that "all have sinned, and come short of the glory of God" (Romans 3:23). Only one person ever lived a life of perfect sinlessness—Jesus, He "was in all points tempted like as we are, yet without sin" (Hebrews 4:15).

So why does the Catholic Church teach that Mary never sinned? Simply because if Jesus was sinless, then they feel that His mother had to be sinless. But it is a mistake to assume that just because Jesus' mother was a sinner, He had to be born a sinner. You see, Jesus received from His mother a body "in the likeness of sinful flesh" (Romans 8:3). But He received from His Father a divine spirit and mind. Jesus' body, degraded by the effects of four thousand years of sin, did not control His actions or sully His character. Though His sinful flesh provided a launching pad for temptation, His divine nature recoiled from it. He chose not to heed temptation's slightest whisper. Therefore, He was without sin.

If Jesus had been born of a sinless mother, then He couldn't be the sympathizing Savior that He is. It is because He did receive "the likeness of sinful flesh" from Mary that He is "touched with the feeling of our infirmities" (Hebrews 4:15). He is our Mediator and heavenly Priest by virtue of this very fact. He understands us because He was tempted from His flesh. "Wherefore in all things it behooved him to be made like unto his brethren, that he might be a merciful and faithful high priest in things pertaining to God, to make reconciliation for the sins of the people. For in that he himself suffered being tempted, he is able to succour them that are tempted" (Hebrews 2:17, 18).

The Immaculate Conception veils the compassion of Jesus. This is why Mary is often prayed to as a mediator and intercessor. Catholic catechisms portray her as one who understands our weaknesses better than Christ. "She is our Mother, near and dear to us, loving us with all the warmth of a mother's love. As the little child frightened by the shadows of night finds safety in his mother's arms, so will we in time of temptation find a safe refuge by fleeing to the outstretched arms of Mary our Mother. If we will but clasp the loving hand of our Mother, stretched out to aid us in every danger, our uncertain footsteps will be guided safely to that golden ladder upon whose rungs we will climb step by step, to the very throne of her Son and Savior, Jesus Christ."[41]

The Catholic teaching of the Assumption of Mary is another area of concern. This declares that Mary was taken to heaven before her body decomposed in the grave. "It was eminently fitting that the body of the chaste and Immaculate Mother of God was not permitted to undergo disintegration and putrefaction but was assumed into heaven."[42]

Given the burial process in Bible days, this would have had to happen very soon after her death. Four days after Lazarus' death, his sisters expected his dead body would be decomposed. "By this time he stinketh: for he hath been dead four days" (John 11:39). Therefore, according to Catholic teaching, for Mary not to "undergo disintegration and putrefaction" we must .conclude she was taken to heaven within four days.

Again the Bible does not teach this. It is a new doctrine of the Catholic Church. "This belief ... was formally defined as a dogma of the Universal Church by Pope Pius XII on November 1, 1950."[43] Instead, the Bible declares that all who die go to the grave to sleep in the dust until the return of Christ. "And many of them that sleep in the dust of the earth shall awake, some to everlasting life, and some to shame and everlasting contempt" (Daniel 12:2; see also Ecclesiastes 9:5,10; Psalms 146:4; 13:3).

Catholics need to re-examine their doctrines concerning Mary. Good Catholic Christians who love God and who've been taught to have an emotional attachment to

Mary may find objectivity difficult. But if they will keep Jesus foremost in their hearts and minds they will be able to extricate this unbiblical doctrine from their prayers and lives. And they will be infinitely more blessed. All the love and devotion they've felt for Mary will now be available for the Savior. Here they will find a richer, fuller experience far beyond anything they've yet known.

Conclusion

One Presbyterian pastor described himself as "a Presbyterian by earthquake." You see, years ago his grandmother moved from Iowa to California. It wasn't long before the local Presbyterian pastor called to invite her to attend his church. "I'm a Baptist," his grandmother said, "and it will take an act of God to get me to change." Remarkably, just at that moment an earthquake shook the home. This farm girl from the Iowa plains had never felt anything like this before. Trembling, she told the pastor, "I'll join."

Christians sometimes choose their church affiliation for strange reasons. But once they've found a church home, most people cling to it tenaciously. "I was born a member of this church and I will die a member," is sometimes the motto. While it is good that we cling to our Christian faith, we must be more open to denominational change if we are ever to answer Jesus' prayer for His people to be one.

All Christians need to strive for unity. But we must unite on the platform of Bible truth. Anything less than honest adherence to truth minimizes the teachings of Scripture to justify each denomination's highly cherished traditions.

It is good that the pope is confessing his church's sins and errors. Protestants need to do the same. But then we all need to go beyond confession. There must be change. We must give up any doctrine and practice not in harmony with Scripture.

This will not be easy. We may feel a little like the farmer who was out one day on his tractor when he rolled over several gopher mounds. The earth caved in under his tire and the tractor flipped. Fortunately, he was only bruised in the accident. His wife gave a great sigh of relief when she heard of his brush with danger and said to him, "Honey, the Lord sure was with you." Looking at his bruises, the farmer replied, "Well, if He was, He sure got a rough ride." Some days we may feel as though the Lord is taking us on a rough ride. Returning to Bible truth and surrendering cherished opinions and unbiblical doctrines may feel painful.

We all have a special challenge ahead of us. In spite of the personal pain we may feel, we must follow our love for Jesus into a more complete obedience to His Word. Let neither Protestants nor Catholics allow themselves to be seduced into any arrangement under the banner of unity that compromises the Bible. None should yield on this point. Hundreds of thousands of men, women, boys, and girls have shed their blood in ancient days because they would not compromise. If we abandon truth now, we will walk through the blood of these dear believers who chose death over compromise.

God is drawing His people back together Those who live up to all the teachings of God's Word are called the "remnant" in the Bible "The dragon was wroth with the woman and went to make war with the remnant o her seed, which keep the commandments of God, and have the testimony of Jesus Christ" (Revelation 12:17). God's remnant people are identified by their fidelity to His commandments and Bible truth. People from all religious backgrounds will eventually unite to make up this loyal group that loves Jesus supremely.

So, how can you guarantee your place in this remnant? Pursue Bible truth relentlessly. Then obey it with just as much gusto. And do it because you love Jesus. As each of us is faithful to God's Word, we can participate in fulfilling this prophecy. Then we can truly have an uncompromised world church that answers Jesus' prayer for unity.

Endnotes

1 Alan Abramsky, Life in These United States, *Reader's Digest,* January 1996, p. 60.

2 Jack Kelley, "Pope Asks Forgiveness of Church's Sins," *USA Today,* May 22, 1995.

3 *Ibid.*

4 Pope John Paul II's "Orientale Lumen," letter dated May 2, 1995. (Quoted in "Pope Wants To Forgive, Forget Schism With Eastern Churches," *San Francisco Chronicle,* May 3, 1995, page A11.)

5 Kelley, *USA Today,* May 22, 1995.

6 Pope John Paul II's "Orientale Lumen," letter dated May 2, 1995.

7 Pope John Paul II, "Ut Unum Sint."

8 Pope John Paul II, *Crossing the Threshold of Hope* (New York: Alfred A. Knopf, 1994), p. 151.

9 Kelley, *USA Today,* May 22, 1995.

10 Pope John Paul II, "Ut Unum Sint."

11 John A. Hardon, S.J., *The Question and Answer Catholic Catechism* (Garden City, NY: Image Books, 1981), p. 37.

12 Philip Schaff, *History of the Christian Church,* vol. 6, p. 306.

13 Heinrich Julius Holtzmann, *Kanon und Tradition* ("Canon and Tradition"), (Ludwigsburg: Druck und Verlad Von Ferd. Riehm, 1859), p. 263.

14 John Henry Newman, *An Essay On the Development of Christian Doctrine,* (London: Longmans, Green & Company, 1906), pp. 372, 373.

15 Rev. John A. O'Brien, *The Faith of Millions,* (Huntington, IN: Our Sunday Visitor, Inc., 1974), Revised edition, pp. 136, 137.

16 *Ibid.,* pp. 110, 111.

17 John A. Hardon, S,J., *The Question and Answer Catholic Catechism,* p. 101.

18 Pope John Paul II, "Ut Unum Sint."

19 Father Gerald Williams, *The Contemporary Catholic Catechism,* (Des Plaines, IL: Fare, Inc., 1973), p. 156.

20 John A. Hardon, S.J., *The Question and Answer Catholic Catechism,* p. 264.

21 Rev. William J. Cogan, *A Catechism for Adults,* (Chicago, IL: Adult Catechetical Teaching Aids Foundation, 1975), p. 78.

22 *Ibid.*

23 *Ibid.,* p. 80.

24 Rev. John P. Scholl, *A New Catechism of the Catholic Faith,* (Des Plaines, IL: Fare, Inc., Revised 1978), p. 62.

25 John A. Hardon, S.J., *The Question and Answer Catholic Catechism,* p. 294.

26 Father Gerald Williams, *The Contemporary Catholic Catechism,* p. 158.

27 Lewis Grizzard, *Chili Dawgs Always Bark at Night,* (New York: Villard Books, 1989), p. 53.

28 Megan Goldin, *The Sacramento Bee,* August 28, 1995, p. A6.

29 John A. Hardon, S.J., *The Question and Answer Catholic Catechism,* p. 244.

30 *Ibid.,* p. 245.

31 *Ibid.,* p. 246.

32 *Ibid.,* p. 245.

33 Father Gerald Williams, *The Contemporary Catholic Catechism,* p. 123.

34 Ian Frazier, *Great Plains* (New York: Farrar/ Straus/Giroux, 1989), pp. 67–69.

35 Rev. John A. O'Brien, *The Faith of Millions,* p. 365.

36 Rev. William J. Cogan, *A Catechism for Adults,* p. 140.

37 *Ibid.*

38 John A. Hardon, S.J., *The Question and Answer Catholic Catechism,* p. 321.

39 Rev. John A. O'Brien, *The Faith of Millions,* pp. 367, 368.

40 *Ibid.,* p. 368.

41 *Ibid.,* pp. 372, 373.

42 *Ibid.,* p. 368.

43 *Ibid.*